I0828194

THIS BOOK BELONGS TO:

WELCOME
TO
MAINE

DIRIGO
MAINE

Dedicated to all the explorers.

ISBN 978-1-958985-88-5

www.joeysavestheday.com

A Mimi Book

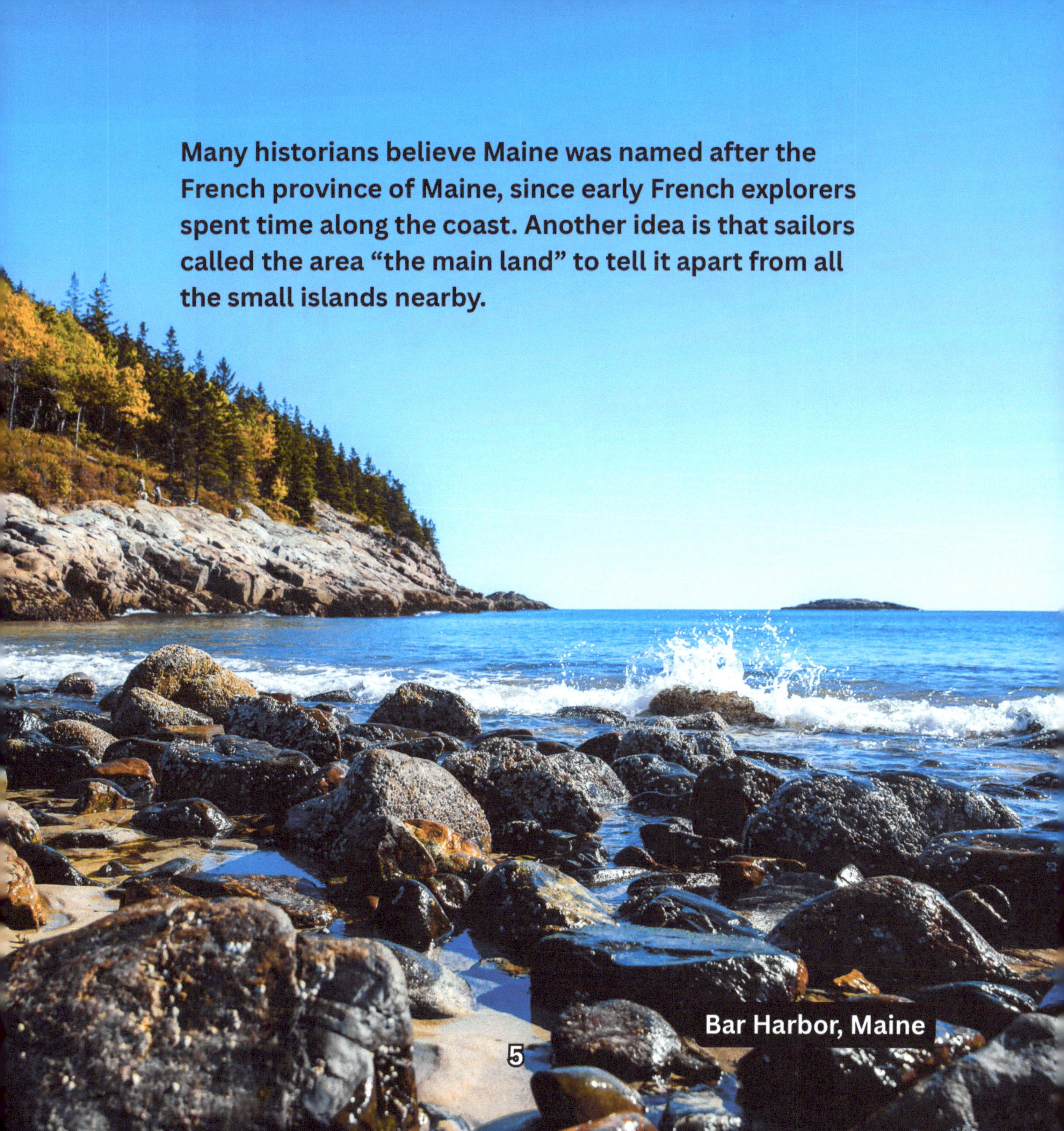

Many historians believe Maine was named after the French province of Maine, since early French explorers spent time along the coast. Another idea is that sailors called the area "the main land" to tell it apart from all the small islands nearby.

Bar Harbor, Maine

Maine's history stretches back thousands of years, beginning with the Wabanaki peoples, who lived in the region long before Europeans arrived. They built strong communities, traveled by canoe, and cared for the forests, rivers, and coastline. In the 1600s, French and English settlers came to the area, building trading posts and small towns. For many years, Maine was actually part of Massachusetts, and life here was shaped by fishing, shipbuilding, and the rugged wilderness.

Maine was the twenty-third state to join the Union. It officially joined on March 15, 1820.

Maine is located in the northeastern United States and sits in the region known as New England. The only state it shares a border with is New Hampshire.

Augusta is the capital of Maine.
It officially became the capital in 1827.

Augusta, Maine, has an estimated population of about 19,000 people, making it one of the smallest state capitals in the United States.

Maine is the thirty-ninth largest state in the United States by area, making it one of the smaller states in size but the biggest in all of New England.

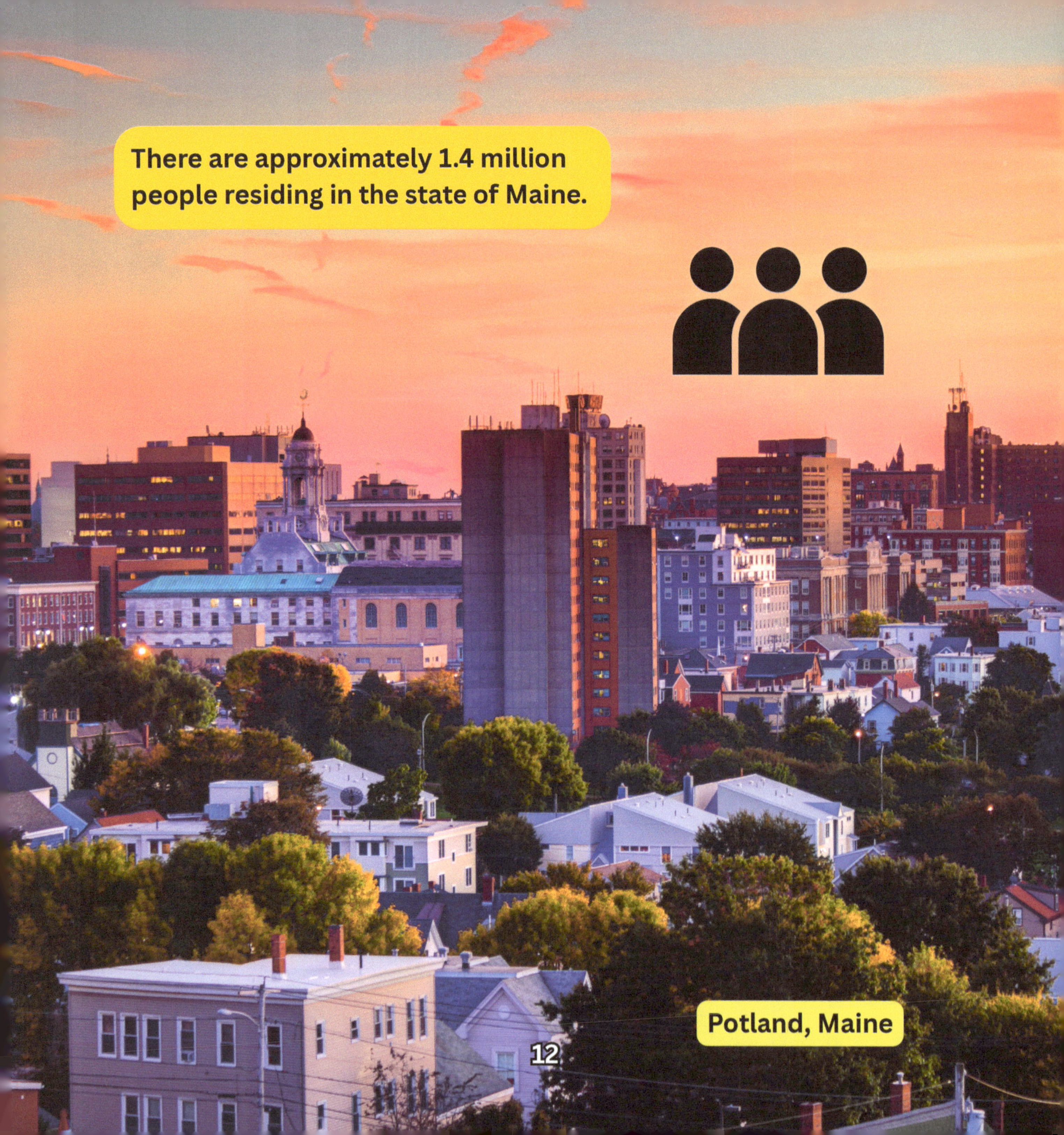

There are approximately 1.4 million people residing in the state of Maine.

Potland, Maine

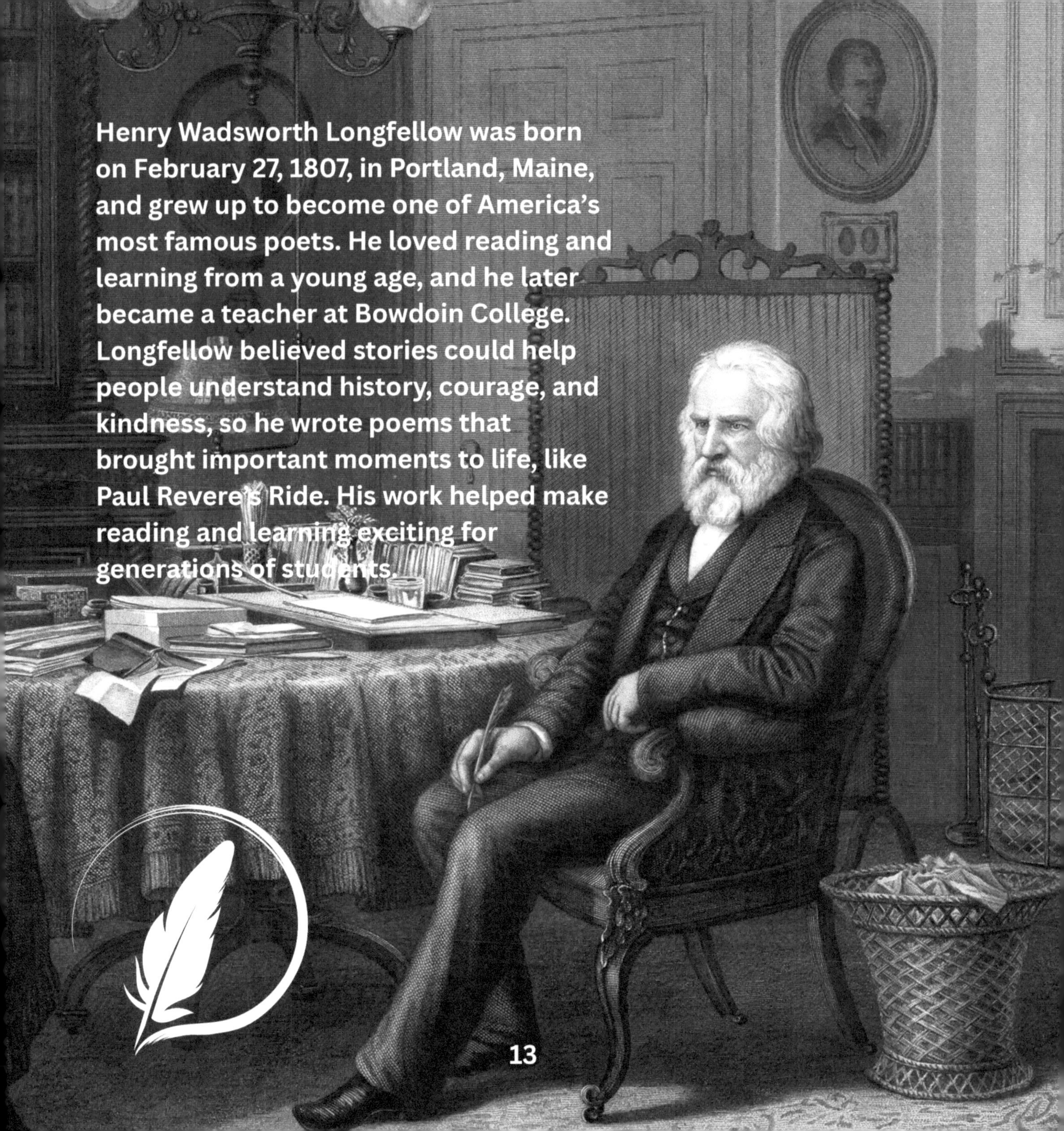

Henry Wadsworth Longfellow was born on February 27, 1807, in Portland, Maine, and grew up to become one of America's most famous poets. He loved reading and learning from a young age, and he later became a teacher at Bowdoin College. Longfellow believed stories could help people understand history, courage, and kindness, so he wrote poems that brought important moments to life, like Paul Revere's Ride. His work helped make reading and learning exciting for generations of students.

Blueberry pie is one of Maine's most beloved treats, made with the tiny, sweet wild blueberries that grow all across the state. These berries are smaller than regular blueberries, but they're packed with flavor, which makes the pie extra delicious. Families in Maine have been baking blueberry pies for generations, especially in the summer when the berries are ripe. Because wild blueberries are such an important part of Maine's history and culture, blueberry pie was chosen as the official state dessert.

Maine

There are 16 counties in Maine.

Here is a list of those counties:

Androscoggin
Aroostook
Cumberland
Franklin
Hancock
Kennebec
Knox
Lincoln
Oxford
Penobscot
Piscataquis
Sagadahoc
Somerset
Waldo
Washington
York

Moxie Falls is one of Maine's most famous and beautiful waterfalls. It's located near the small town of The Forks, deep in the state's forested wilderness. The waterfall drops nearly 90 feet, making it one of the tallest in New England. A wooden boardwalk leads visitors through the trees to viewing platforms where they can watch the water rush over the cliff and into the clear pool below.

90 FEET

Portland Head Light is one of the most photographed lighthouses in the entire world, and it sits on a rocky cliff in Cape Elizabeth, watching over the Atlantic Ocean. It's the oldest lighthouse in Maine, first lit in 1791, and it still shines its bright beam to help ships find their way safely along the coast.

1892

The Androscoggin Swinging Bridge is a special footbridge that stretches across the Androscoggin River, connecting the towns of Brunswick and Topsham in southern Maine. It was first built in 1892 so mill workers could walk safely across the river to get to work each day.

The Maine state bird is the Black-capped Chickadee. It was chosen as the state bird in 1927.

The official state flower of Maine is the White Pine Cone and Tassel. It was chosen as the state flower in 1895.

Maine is commonly referred to as the Pine Tree State.

The Pine Tree State!

Maine's state motto is "Dirigo," which means "I lead." It was officially adopted in 1820 when Maine became a state.

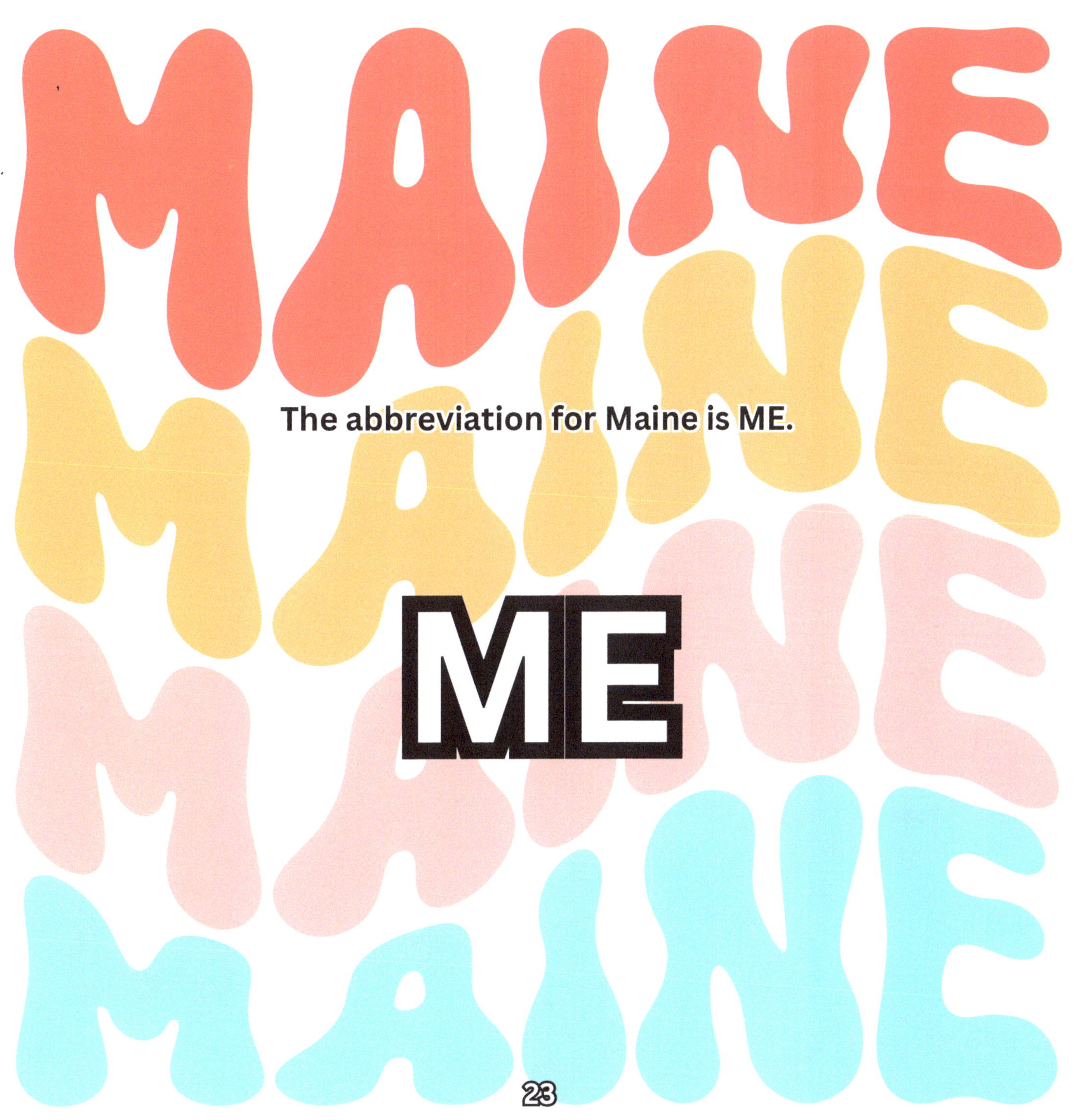

The abbreviation for Maine is ME.

ME

Maine's state flag was officially adopted in 1909.

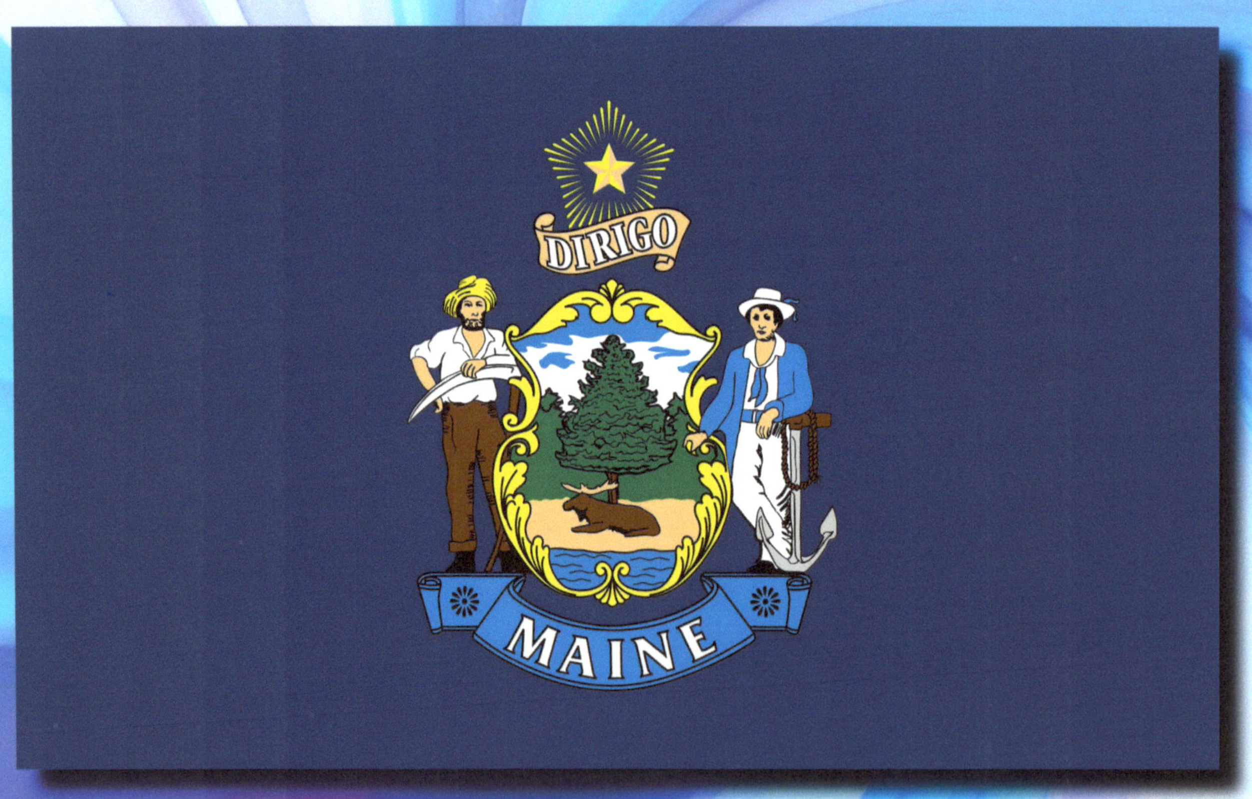

Some crops grown in Maine are blueberries, barley, tomatoes, potatoes, apples, and carrots.

Some animals that live in Maine are moose, river otters, striped skunks, puffins, and blackbears.

Maine experiences wide temperature swings throughout the year. The hottest temperature ever recorded in the state was 105°F, measured in North Bridgton on July 10, 1911. On the opposite end, Maine's coldest temperature was −50°F, recorded in Big Black River on January 16, 2009.

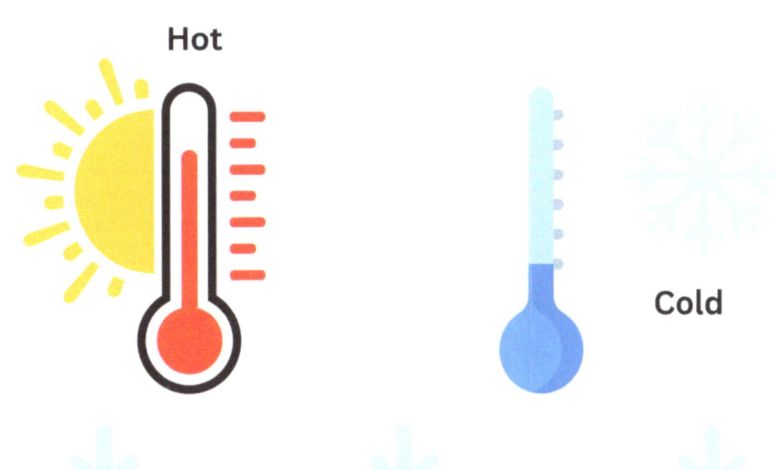

The Maine Wildlife Park in Gray is home to many of the animals that live in Maine's forests and mountains. Kids can see moose, black bears, lynx, bobcat, deer, along with owls, eagles, and other colorful birds. The park focuses on animals that are native to the state, making it a fun place for families to learn about Maine's wildlife together.

Acadia National Park is one of Maine's most magical places, where mountains, forests, and the ocean all meet in one stunning landscape. Families can explore rocky beaches, quiet ponds, and miles of scenic trails. Kids love climbing on the pink granite rocks, spotting tide-pool creatures, and watching the waves crash against the cliffs.

The largest airport in Maine is the Portland International Jetport, located in Portland, in the southern part of the state. It sits at 1001 Westbrook Street, Portland, Maine, and serves as the main travel hub for people flying in and out of Maine. The Jetport connects travelers to cities across the country and is known for its easy layout, friendly atmosphere, and cozy Maine feel.

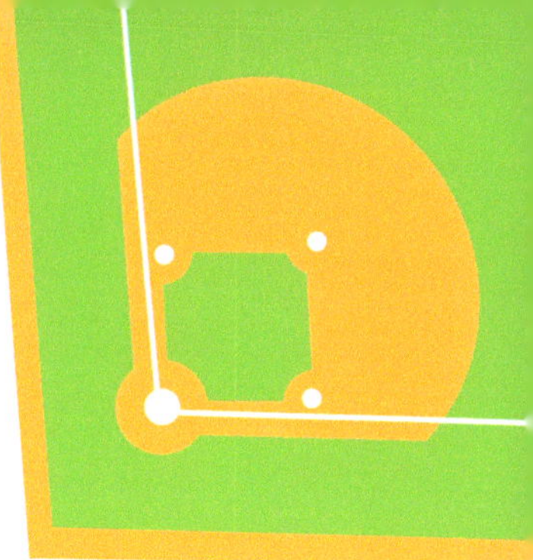

The Portland Sea Dogs are a Minor League Baseball team based in Portland, right along the city's busy waterfront. They play their home games at Hadlock Field, a cheerful ballpark known for its family-friendly atmosphere and its famous "Maine Monster" left-field wall. The Sea Dogs are the Double-A affiliate of the Boston Red Sox, which means many future major-league players spend time on this team as they develop their skills.

FOOTBALL

The University of Maine Black Bears are the most well-known football team in the state, and they play in Orono, in the central part of Maine. Their home field is Alfond Stadium, a lively place where fans bundle up in blue and white to cheer on the team. The Black Bears are known for their tough, spirited play and the strong sense of community that fills the stadium on game days, making each matchup feel like a true Maine tradition.

The white pine is Maine's state tree. It stays green all year and grows tall and graceful, giving Maine's forests their fresh, woodsy smell. White pines have soft, flexible needles and long, slender cones, and they've played an important role in Maine's history. Their strong, straight trunks were once prized for ship masts and helped build homes, towns, and traditions all across the state.

The landlocked salmon is Maine’s state fish. It’s a sleek, silver fish known for its strong swimming and graceful leaps as it travels through Maine’s cold lakes and rivers. Even though it’s powerful, the landlocked salmon is gentle and spends most of its time gliding through clear waters in search of smaller fish.

Can you name these?
DIRIGO
MAINE

I hope you enjoyed
learning about
Maine.

To explore fun facts about the other 49 states, visit my website at www.joeysavestheday.com. You'll also find a wide variety of homeschool resources to support joyful learning at home. If you enjoyed this book, I would be grateful if you left a review. Your feedback truly helps. Thank you for your support!

Check out these other interesting books in the 50 States Fact Books Series!

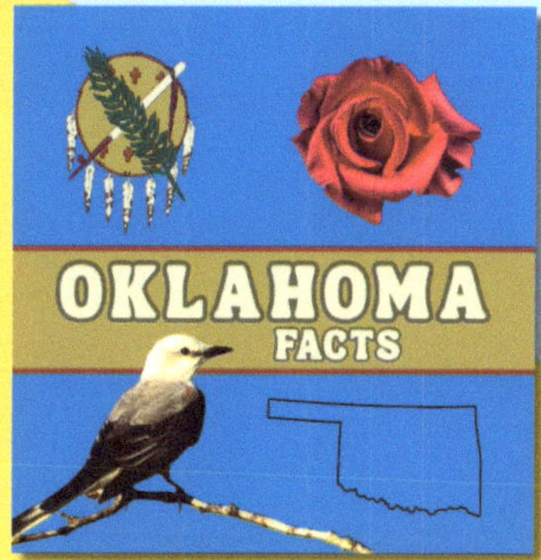

www.mimibooks.com

www.ingramcontent.com/pod-product-compliance
Lightning Source LLC
LaVergne TN
LVHW070200110826
845147LV00002B/455
* 9 7 8 1 9 5 8 9 8 5 8 8 5 *